Blaze

Blaze

poems by
PEGGY SHUMAKER

paintings by
KESLER E. WOODWARD

Red Hen Press Los Angeles

Blaze

Poems copyright © 2005 by Peggy Shumaker
Paintings copyright © 2005 by Kesler E. Woodward

ALL RIGHTS RESERVED

No part of this book may be used or reproduced in any manner whatever without the prior written permission of both the publisher and the copyright owner.

Peggy Shumaker photo credit Barry McWayne
Kesler E. Woodward photo credit Robert Peck, Philadelphia Academy of Natural Sciences
Book and cover design by Mark E. Cull
Layout assistance: Michael Vukadinovich and Evan Schnair

ISBN: 1-59709-053-0 (tradepaper)
ISBN: 1-59709-054-9 (casebound)
Library of Congress Catalog Card Number: 2005930960

Published by Red Hen Press

The City of Los Angeles Cultural Affairs Department, California Arts Council, Los Angeles County Arts Commission and National Endowment for the Arts partially support Red Hen Press.

First Edition
Printed in Canada

for Len and Jo Braarud

CONTENTS

paintings

Graces	12
A Sapling for Heather	14
Couple	16
Untitled #6	18
Bright Birches in Winter	20
Melt	22
Birch Portrait #19	24
Birch Bark, St. Matthew	26
Birch Portrait #30	28
Birch Portrait, Homer	30
Birch Portrait #33	32
Bright Birch, Deep Winter	34
Untitled #4	36
Bright Birch	38
Little Gidding	40
Spring Green	42
Birch Portrait #29	44
Birch Portrait #35	46
Summer Birch	48
Birch Portrait #32	50
Chena Birch	52
Bright Birch #2	54
Birch Portrait #31	56

poems

The Trees Won't Notice	13
Blazes	15
Couple	17
Strong Stars	19
An Intimacy	21
Melt	23
First Winter: Joy	25
Birch Bark, St. Matthew	27
Six Days of Rain	29
Clitoris	31
Three Notes from a Wooden Flute	33
Still	35
Matisse's Antoinette	37
Rime	39
Elegy for Getz	41
The Day the Leaves Came	43
Exit Glacier	45
Walker Lake	47
Grace	49
Chatanika	51
Cliffside Could Collapse at Any Time	53
Glacier, Calving	55
Just This Once	57

First Snow, September	58	Before Leaves Fall, Snow	59
Northern September	60	Early Fall	61
September Light	62	Too Soon After Rain	63
Birch Portrait #64	64	Kus-sun-ar	65
Triple Birch Portrait	66	Parallel Universes	67
Burnt Norton	68	Once You Name It	69
Birch Portrait #22	70	Braided River	71
Birch Portrait #62	72	The Told Secret	73
Birch Portrait #20	74	Swans, Where We Don't Expect Them	75
Birch Portrait #61	76	Waking to Rain	77
Seasons of Praise: Spring	78		
Seasons of Praise: Summer	78		
Seasons of Praise: Autumn	79		
Seasons of Praise: Winter	79		
Bright Birch #3	80	After Long Drought	81
Bold Birch	82	Absence of Ocean	83
Chimera	84	Refuge	85
Little Birch Portrait	86	Pomegranates	87
Birch Portrait #18	88	God Gestures	89
Snow Up On Birches	90	October, Snow	91
Harriman Birches	92	Short History of One Hour's Desire	93
Bright Birch #1	94	How They Are With Each Other	95
Woods at Creamer's	96	What to Count On	97
Birch Portrait #50	98	Haul Road	99
Birch Portrait #15	100	Each Rise, Each Hollow	101

Fall Fever	102	What Will Remain	103
Bright Birch #4	104	Young Boy Dancing at Playa los Muertos	105
Birch Portrait #41	106	A Crack in the Balanced Ship	107
Birch Portrait #10	108	Censored	109
Birch Portrait #25	110	Maybe	111
Birch Portrait #45	112	Spawn	113
Chase's Woods	114	Chena Night	115
Anniversary	116	Anniversary	117
Birch Portrait #14	118	The Run Of Silvers	119
New Fires	120	Again, Again	121
Birch Portrait #17	122		
Birch Portrait #21	124		
Birch Portrait #28	126		
Birch Portrait #47	128		
Tanana Birch Portrait	130		
Blue Bark Peels	132		
Seasons of Praise: Spring	134	Spring	135
Seasons of Praise: Summer	136	Summer	137
Seasons of Praise: Autumn	138	Autumn	139
Seasons of Praise: Winter	140	Winter	141
Close Set Birches	142	Wide Icy River	143
Birch Portrait #34	144		
East Coker	146	Blaze	147
Birch Portrait #1	148	The Longest Night of the Year	149

Blaze

THE TREES WON'T NOTICE

Trees have their own lives,
branching out each season
to catch and release

light—pure light or light
sifted through smoke, the edges
gorgeous, the burning forest.

The trees won't notice
how they touch us,
how our whole world

is named for one turn—
universe—cosmic laughter
raining steady

till the river rises.
To the painter
standing half a brush-length

away, this canvas becomes
the world, ridges of true
red crashing into violet

devastating and creating
continent, basin, range.
The messy precision

of making
love in all its glory
and beaver dam confusion

purposeful, passionate,
a matter of survival
each chewed trunk

living, then giving
life beyond its own
verso, recto

leaves turning,
the place where bark's
peeled back

complexion freshly scrubbed
the deliberate smear
layer upon layer

laid down wet
as the free and unmerited favor
of...well, maybe god

maybe the edge
of the not-yet
imagined

maybe the force
of the made thing.

BLAZES

Wounds we inflict
on white bark of a birch
to show those who follow
which way
we passed. Cut deep enough
to show us
maybe the way home.

White wash down the face of a sorrel mare
loping toward but missing
the box canyon.

Flash from the muzzles of well-oiled rifles
held to three generations of shoulders, aimed
always at what we bring down.

Flares in the forest, where grime-smeared
fighters stoop over Pulaskis, chopping
smolders out of earth, the charred ground
exhaling second-hand smoke,
smoke in their faces,
ash settling for weeks, that bad dream
you can't shake,
dream of not breathing, buried,
deeper than light,
deeper than restless earth, deeper
than spirits still passionate without bodies,
deeper than any way out.

COUPLE

After so many seasons
frost, hard winter, break up,
buds, after ripe summer
dwindling, frost . . .

After so many seasons,
if wind and water
were to conspire,
loosen and lift them

so the splendor
of their roots
rose up in front of
God and everybody

who could know
how they knew
each other, who could
sort through

which tangle fed
the one whose bark
caught sun every morning,
which snarl

slaked thirst
for the one evening stoked.
Who could tell
after so many seasons

so many wounds
hardened, so many skins
outgrown, so many
splits, so many

leaves quaking
gone gold
then gone
all together.

After so many seasons
when that smoky wind
roused them to claw
each other's eyes out

who could tell
when one stopped wanting
and the other began
who could know

when crosswind breezes
might lift their pollen
to drift over the river,
carried away, relieved.

STRONG STARS

Mottled grouse peck
    up gizzard stones
        before the first snow—

seasons move on
    as if the human heart were not
        infinitely fragile.

The sow bear's stained snout lifts,
    sniffs the wind, then bows
        to claws raking in

stems, berries, rasping leaves.
    A twelve-year-old, pleased, tells her aunt
        I kissed a boy four times and my tooth

grew back in.
    Beside the barrow ditch, the bandy-legged fox
        bounds into finger-thin willow.

Strong stars surround the green
    wash of the aurora, God's love, the moisture
        of a woman's orgasm

From here, we can see much farther
    than we can walk.
        We walk to the edges of our bodies.

AN INTIMACY

Falling
    and already
        fallen

May snow
    lights
        on tufts of moss

dusting
    the bizarre
        upholstery

springing from
    juts and crannies
        broken edges

where the birches'
    many-layered bodies
        have split, scrolled back

and left wide open
    the unblemished
        inner self.

A tinge
    of light-washed pink
        draws one to touch

the translucent ear
    of an infant,
        the open thighs

of a happy woman
    walking
        naked.

MELT

Sun-warmed cedar planks—
        the scent of spruce and peeling birch—
                your mouth finds mine, we turn

from the porch rail
        to take this journey of tongues—
                a shiver of moisture

the natural spring
        rainwater under snow
                a shimmer in the hollow.

FIRST WINTER: JOY

Yesterday at ten below
we tried to hang a birdfeeder
to the lowest strong branch
of the birch outside the big window.

I held the little redwood
chalet by one eave.
He bent, and tucked his head
between my thighs, lifted me

laughing high enough to loop
blue filaments of fishing leader
into crooks in the bark.
Spilt seed nestled in his curls.

I tied one knot. By then,
my earlobes had stopped hurting.
The fingers in my gloves
weren't taking orders.

So I trussed it up
best I could, and we
ran, remembering why kids run
everywhere, back inside.

This morning, the seed
has all drained away,
a perfect heap in the snow,
the glass house
dangling by one corner.

BIRCH BARK, ST. MATTHEW

Matthew 7: 7

Ask,   your life   a stone
       dropped in a pond   questions
           circling

Seek,
        and where you've yet to look
       that's where
          your soul   hides

Knock, and
       shadows
       may answer

Ask,
       thirst
       for unquenchable flames

Seek what you have
          no way to take in

Knock, and your body
       will crack
       open, ovum
       of light

SIX DAYS OF RAIN

River so high
veiled beekeepers
smoke-stun honeymakers,
lift hives to dry ground.

River so swollen
beaver don't even try
to sweep upstream
with mouths full of birch.

River so fast
whole trunks of birch
root wads and branches
ram downstream,

batter floatplanes,
piers, scatter lodges
beavers spent all season
mounding for winter.

River so driven
its own body's
not the body
it wore this morning.

CLITORIS

Surely a man named it.

If a woman had chosen, we'd
have hawk tongue, pearl
of flame, olala berry,
suck nubbin, jujube
tsunami.

THREE NOTES FROM A WOODEN FLUTE

A moon with two points
cradles chill mist.
Where you are,
can you see it?

Moist starlight on new moss—
flannel blue, a melting
snow ridge

I care for this birch bud
so tightly wrapped
in itself
it seems solid

One passing shadow
          a trickle at the root—
a hush of breath
          along the unclothed limb—

it will somehow know
          to open

STILL

Too cold to snow, too cold
to catch a second curl
of smoky green aurora before
toes harden into icy stones.
Solid, the river, still
the cloudless sky.

A single breath lifts
clouds of powder. The cow moose
wanders close, leans
toward logs we live in, lingers
under eaves where she can reach
without wading shoulder deep
to prune tips of willow, to strip
with hooves and aching teeth
tough living bark.

MATISSE'S ANTOINETTE

Because they are truly her friends, they leave her
tasting salt in her dreams, salt and green lemons.
Cool porcelain, a windowsill, vanilla and wax.
Her friends leave her
flowers, and tied to the flowers, a note
scratched on butcher paper. Blue-black gentian
folded in a green wax cone. Their last cut hours
sweated out formally, each stem
arranged in the swirl-glazed tureen.

In the bath, she stretches full-length—
two bruised red peonies surface.
Because she did not love him, she allowed
one young man to stroke the sleek slope
of her hip, wondering what he would find
to possess, what she had
to parcel, what one
needs must conserve, always. How little
it has to do with the body.

RIME

Overnight, each twig has grown
white fur, the air so still
snow throws
into sharp relief each
branch plus
each branch's crooked
light-bent sense
of self, crystallized.
Last night, your voice
roused my limbs,
warm under flannel,
licked each branch,
split, & hollow,
licked into flame the untamed
liquids, flammable, spilled
down your chin,
moisture from the heart-
wood, risen unseasonably,
springing free not just from me,
nor your snow-cloud
juices just from you,
no—these waters
rise from hot springs
at the center of the sacred,
from the little stone
overlooked, often,
plain little stone
where vibrations from each life
ever lived, each life
yet to be, gather.

ELEGY FOR GETZ

Rough tongue, wet reed, a working girl's heel
lithe blood, nude bricks, a sorcerer's creel

A cantaloupe's grin as flesh slips from the shell
A ditch digger's bossa, the favela's smells

A samba's raw onion sliced into threes
A mouthful of light released on the sea

Dirt road, raw skin, the ocean on fire
Curved claw, spiked toad, cool lizard desire

The torturer's daughter, the disappeared's shoe
Fresh bruises that throb, it's the blood, it's the blood

Old tracks, black beans, the birth water's gush
Chipped tooth, hot nails, a bolt of caçhaca

A tongue touch of sweat on a bare collarbone
Red dance of that horse, a slingshot stone

Bright horn, brief life, brass tunnel of scars
Each breath, cracked seed, blown pollen of stars

THE DAY THE LEAVES CAME

For so long the hillside shone white,
the white of white branches laden, the sky
more white, the river unmoved.

And when the first stirrings started
underneath, the hollowing subtle,
unpredictable, rotten crust gave way—

ice water up to the ankle! She
turned from her work and shook
her wet foot. The buds had broken.

Not the green of birches in full leaf.
Not meadow, tundra, berry patch, tussock.
For this moment only, this green—

the touch of one loved
in secret, a gasp held in,
let go.

EXIT GLACIER

When we got close enough
we could hear

rivers inside the ice
heaving splits

the groaning of a ledge
about to

calve. Strewn in the moraine
fresh moose sign—

tawny oblong pellets
breaking up

sharp black shale. In one breath,
ice and air—

                                                  history, the record
                                                  of breaking—

                                                  prophecy, the warning
                                                  of what's about to break

                                                  out from under
                                                  four stories

                                                  of bone-crushing turquoise,
                                                  retreating.

WALKER LAKE

The sow bear ripped
down the boat tarp,
scraped black fur

into twisted wingnuts,
that bear
eased her itch and disappeared.

And still she stayed near,
while we hiked
uphill to fill our jug,

the spring covered over
with autumn's leavings.
We skimmed clear

frosted growth floating,
sank our jerrycans,
felt them pull deeper.

The surface healed
around wrists
stiff with cold.

Bubbles shook free
from river weeds, rose up,
tumbled downstream.

The still place returned
to reflection. Birch
startled us with gold

so loud our bodies
flared like fireweed
gone to seed.

Twilight
put its slant
on the afternoon—

four loons
swam near
our seaplane,

nudging this
strange relative
who would not speak.

The moon had eaten itself
down to the rind,
and in that sliver,

that lingering
of autumn, stars borrowed
the voices of loons.

GRACE

When light stretches
from what we call
yesterday to what we call
tomorrow, the smallest
winged ones who winter over
tuck seeds in the peeled-back
scrolls of paper birch,
sunflower and millet they'll revisit
in the last gasp of light
iced over at forty below,

black capped and boreal
whisks skimming
spruce needles, skimming
last birch buds—
stylized grace
no gesture wasted,
women bending in kimono—
ancient refinement—survival's
ceremony green, startling,
frothy tea.

CHATANIKA

High, the Chatanika,
high this year, surges
the flats, soaks
the valley. Chatanika

spreads wide
where gravel braids.
Where banks
snug close,

where rock,
earth, and root
gang up, high water
scours, carves,

its own image
changeable.
Chatanika, in pools
deep green, in eddies

steeped tea, freezes
and thaws, makes its way on,
full of grayling
flashing like thoughts

among the millions
of mirrors at Minto.
*What brought me
exactly here?*

*Is my flowing
through the world
a fit gift? Have I nourished
more roots than I undercut?*

CLIFFSIDE COULD COLLAPSE AT ANY TIME

Tonight no casual sorrow
consoles us. Tonight

our bodies reteach us
that they too

brine and bone-churning
breakers

live as water held in
by membranes

elastic as kinship,
as love-time, as skin—

surface tension
constant

only so long—
then the gush

birth rush
and we're blinking

in a world
that won't come into focus

for quite some time,
we're depending

again on the kindness
of strangers stranger and stranger

strangers we name water, earth,
mother, lover, father, daughter, son . . .

GLACIER, CALVING

Kachemak Bay, Alaska

We picked through shoulder high
wide blade grasses, listening to the fading
snicker and he-yup of the trainer
posting a skittish foal. The massive
hooves of unshod Morgans turned the soil,
carved hollows to catch timothy seed,
grave half-moons to cradle rain.

A sweet-water stream emptied across rock beach
into Kachemak Bay. Across the way, glaciers
thrust splintered shale into black-shined
moraine, quick rivers charging inside them.
The bay caught the light, threw it back.

Something inside you let go.
You spoke of your father, who never learned to read,
grinding his teeth as you helped his hand
scrawl the letters of his painful name.
You told of the grandmother who wished you
never born, for fear you'd be like him. I held you.
That bitter river coursed.

At sunset we hiked to the rough lumber cabin.
Mud daubers under the eaves
dove for our faces, then banked
and soared over the unfenced field.
All night mosquitoes drilled through sleep—

each slap of little death
awake, and wet, and echoing.

JUST THIS ONCE

Everyone else snores.
Black nets billow, let in

a few mosquitoes.
I sneak out,

careful to prop shut
the cabin door so porcupines

won't be tempted, pull on
hip waders folded knee-high,

head up the path
not singing,

not calling out, not
jangling bells

to warn the one who left
tracks bigger than ours

at the edge of the water
and her spring cub

who dawdled behind, clawing up
storm clouds of silt—

undisturbed and not disturbing
I stand still breathing in

sphagnum's mossy sigh
quiet after loon calls, follow

unmarked paths
left by stars too wild

to show themselves anywhere
but here, inhale

her nursing musk,
the bear

I know
is there.

BEFORE LEAVES FALL, SNOW

Some still green,
        leaves cling,

catch snow loads
        so heavy the birches

bend double. Just one
        tall tree bent

into wire zaps out
        what we call power.

Birch trees take on burdens
        they could never

have predicted, hold on
        too long

to last year's leaves. Interrupted,
        they can't finish

letting go, and so
        they show us

how they suffer. They bow,
        they don't die.

Snow arches, boosted
        by bent wood—

rude cathedrals.
        Gravity and ravens

shake loose
        dry snow.

A lone birch straightens
        toward sky.

Laden birch stay
        bent all winter,

bent always, bow down
        even in full sun

to earth, rich,
        made of birch.

EARLY FALL

Split quarter round
        stove lengths

vanish. Heavy
        snow a shock

to neighbors who thought
        they had a week

maybe two
        to nail down the roof

a shock to the cutter
        who still has four cords

to put by. Early snow
        a thrill

even where winter lasts
        till May.

All day
        light dances,

swirls down,
        alive.

Birches embrace
        what falls

on their shoulders,
        in their laps.

TOO SOON AFTER RAIN

*(Sonoran desert, where the dead
are said to cherish fragrances)*

Too soon after rain blue woman
takes a step toward her mother
long gone, that memory an aroma

of cilantro gathered from
tree wells. Sopa fideo, no bother
so soon after rain. The woman

wants to recall her future. Not the one
she will live, but the dreamt other
long gone, a mother's legacy. This aroma:

a sweaty man, welcome,
pours his skyful of sorrow inside her
too soon. After rain, blue woman

walks, each footprint an omen
shaped in earth, of earth, the mother
not gone. Long memory, that aroma

of death sprouting. Dark humus
feeding us, feeding on us and all others.
Too soon. After rain blue woman's
long gone, like memory. Now, the aroma.

KUS-SUN-AR

For an injured friend,
he brings salmon fillets, fish
he caught dipnetting all night at Chitina.
Needlenose pliers nipped out
all the invisible bones.

Growing up at fish camp, he'd sneeze.
Elders said, "Kus-sun-ar."
Otter. They invoked otter's name
to wish him close
to one who lives in more than one world.
Shaman helper, on land, in water.

He tells me otters live inside women, curled up
just above the stomach,
and this feels true. I feel my otters,
restless, disturbed.

My hurt body can't rest yet,
it was so close to the other world.

I'm an otter, skinned in the round,
my pelt pulled off in one piece.
Stitched into a kit bag,
I feel the shaman placing his healing tools
one by one into my emptiness.

PARALLEL UNIVERSES

Cool as ripe plums
placed among stones in the clear
rushing stream

her voice, his *yes*.
Fully clothed in the awareness
of death

they lay naked
together reaching
with plain human hands

toward what is holy,
their hands giving life
in each gesture, each touch.

Holy. Even the stone
at the center
of the shared fruit

holds fast mystery,
its power intact
whether planted

with reverence
or tossed
back to earth.

ONCE YOU NAME IT

Once you name it grass,
    the new-mown
    aroma will see you through winter.

Once you name it
    hard durum wheat, it will feed
    the world.

Name it & you assume
    you can stop looking. Though *snow*
    shows only one facet
    of flake or storm or bank, *powder*
    one quality of the slope
    we're sliding down.

Once you name it Mozart, you expect it
    to save you.

Once you name it
    it's yours. You've claimed it.
    Now you must tend it, watch it grow
    into its name, then grow
    out of its name, come
    into its own.

Once you name it home, it will live in you
    no matter where you live
    no matter how you live
    as long as you live.

Once you name it enemy, you devote your life to it.

Once you name it friend, it will forgive you.

Once you name it love, you begin not to know.

Name it blood, & you see how you're related.
    It thickens, rich pudding
    after death, after birth.

Name it death and you step toward it, just
    as you did before it
    weighed down the tongue,
    melted like a wafer
    or a mouthful of snow.

Once you name it birth, you breathe
    first breath
    and cry, cry
    for the world you've left, harder
    cry, for the world
    you've come to, wide
    awake, helpless, unclothed
    but for your cloak
    of blood, hungry
    to put it to your mouth,
    that whole world
    you've yet to name.

BRAIDED RIVER

Under the ice, burbot glide
as if giving birth
to silence.

Someone who held the auger straight
drilled clean through
to moving water,

set gear, then hurried home,
chilled blood pulling back
from the surface, circling deeper

toward the center, the sacred.
As all winter the heartwood
holds the gathered birch sap

still. Ours is only one bend
of a wild, braided river.

THE TOLD SECRET

A young woman tells a secret which she has promised
never to reveal. But slyly, so no one might accuse
her of telling, and no one can be sure it was she
who told. So now she has two secrets—the one
she has betrayed, and the fact of her treason.
Over the years, the weights of these intimacies
settle in her knees, which groan and creak and
remind her with a whole repertoire of pains the depths
of her duplicity. Because she cannot move, she gains
a reputation for stability. Troubled people
seek her out, people with unspeakable difficulties.
They confide in her relentlessly, each secret adding
its own specific weight to her body until even
her eyelids can no longer support themselves.
When she has absolutely room for no more, she hands
back an old confidence in exchange for each new one,
a trading of guilt across generations.
The old people's grievous embarrassments
the young take home as party favors.
Early on, this secret woman discovers that Truth in fact
is the greatest lie, so she always and immediately tells
what she sees. Everyone finds her insanely amusing.
In her later years she is much in demand
at dinner parties. One evening
a young woman does not laugh, though
everyone else in the room leans for balance
on the slim arms of potted palms. The old woman
draws the girl away, into the tiled kitchen.
Listen, I have something to tell you.

SWANS, WHERE WE DON'T EXPECT THEM

Tundra swans twine necks
among snowflakes
vanishing into evening's

river. Past break up,
tablecloths of rotten ice
nest along the bank.

Halfway, swan wings
open, then settle in
like second thoughts.

Maybe they flew
north over Minto,
traced halos

over brooding ponds,
saw from far up
without touching

the world is hard
and will stay hard
a while longer.

WAKING TO RAIN

We share
    warm onion tart
        over watercress
            dressed in citrus

walk the wharf
    where pelicans kamikaze
        dive for fish.
           Our breath

translates into mist
    across mountains,
        watercolor wash prepared
            for a single ink stroke.

When we want to know
    how perfect one moment
        in this life
            may be, consider

reading aloud, late,
    in bed, pure laughter,
        where my mouth lingers
            where your hands barely touch

savor how slowly
    we give over to the other
        our world, our time, our selves—
            one moment's

spirit in harmony
    and we rest, joyous
        beside one another
            dream beyond what we remember

wake to clean water
    newly arrived
        for its moment
            on earth.

AFTER LONG DROUGHT

Over Panguitch Lake
       turkey buzzards spiral
              between rays of rain

that fall
       but fail
              to reach earth.

On parched juniper each drop
       ticks, one moment aware
              of all those gone by.

Still desert air, then the torrent
       darkening
              sandstone and shale.

Your lips on my shoulder,
       rain in the desert, rain
              after long drought.

ABSENCE OF OCEAN

> *And hasn't the sea been lent*
> *for a brief time to the earth?*
> *—Neruda*

When the sea pulled away
red rocks lifted. Rippled silt
shimmered under an ancient moon.
Then sun. Many days of fierce, dry breath.
Silt made of itself
ten thousand bowls
broken by their own need
to curl up to the other
and know edges
the ocean could never
fathom.

The desert knows
better than anybody
the necessary absence
of ocean. It doesn't ask
it demands
moisture, salt,
the wisdom of each cell.
Each body a body
of water,
restless, stirring, returning to sky.

REFUGE

When they do not wish to be seen,
herons, great blue, turn themselves into
top branches of huge eucalyptus.

When she needs not to be recognized,
the fence lizard stops breathing
among monkeyflowers' woody stems.

Snowy egrets, when they wish,
turn yellow toes to worms, wiggle
till fish come, inspect their last moments as fish.

The killdeer's complaint, long-legged,
strides over marsh and trail,
traveler bearing news that gets to us.

Because they are so much themselves,
lotus take a breather, draw air
deep to keep themselves buoyant,

draw air clear down to the roots.
The acorn woodpecker puts aside
what the live oak drops.

Even as plumes of brewer saltbush
brush the underside of brown-eyed susans,
the marsh breathes change, change.

When enough rushes crowd in,
when cattails and marsh grass thicken,
when water gives way to root and leaf,

marsh to meadow,
shallow minty roots of sage
will take hold, grow in dust,

draw finches and Anna's hummers,
grow fine-haired leaves that,
luminous, deflect summer.

POMEGRANATES

San Diego, 1944

Once, as a girl, she pulled down
pomegranates, ruddy and overripe,

their dry bells sounding no warning.
A sharp rock between her thighs

broke into each bulb, the thick seed
quickening her tongue. She swallowed

more than once, but could not
in this way finish the fruit.

Too much, always, when the ripe time
returns to us sticky—

her friends gathered and together
they shattered the tidy pyramid,

emptied the shells onto a long tongue
of oilcloth lapping across the back lawn.

Then one by one the uninitiated ran
wonderfully ashamed, and pressed

each new chest chest-first
slishing barely the blushing seed—

they kept on till the seed dried,
then rinsed off, convinced

now they knew lust,
its moment of extravagance,

its secrets
wasteful enough to keep.

GOD GESTURES

The hill disappears a little
each hour.

Birch leaves
break more light every day.

Next week, promise,
fresh salmon & stories,

laughter's holy communion.
In a month,

will we recognize
the one inside us?

Before long,   of matter rushing
stones won't mind   madder inside

claiming us,   able with word, song,
kindred particles   touch to offer

                                                        god gestures—

                                                        Ah, in you I feel
                                                        what will remain

                                                        when all else
                                                        memory body breath

                                                        has gone along

OCTOBER, SNOW

Quiet snow takes on
the shape of black branches
taking on snow.

This low
along the horizon
the sun

seems hurt,
glazes one birch in last light.
First ice

across the Chena edges out
until two sharpnesses
wound each other into binding.

Dry snow gives way
to the slightest urgings. One black seed
ticks through the crust.

SHORT HISTORY OF ONE HOUR'S DESIRE

For the lips of the recording engineer
    moistening each other as the lights bubble up
For the drunken student's breath of cloves
For the staple guns of flamenco heels
For the foreskin slid back over the chewy mushroom of oblivion
For the lupus victim carried to her toilet
For the throb of destruction in the baby's temple
For the deaf cartoonist's nodding fist
For the hiker's last switchback before he froze
For the mask-maker's wall of weathered skulls
For oiled springlets on an athlete's brow
For the Russian priest's daughter, her tangles and
    tangles, her hip-length hair
For the composer's fingers stroking the businesswoman's ankle
For eyes of the safety patrol who knows
    how hunger hollows bones first
For women skiing cross-country to find a place to be naked
For flames centering fine Thai soup
For the singed waitress delivering fried cheese

For the language of touching after long absence
For chicken-scratch dancers under the tamaracks
For molas layering common cloth to brilliance
For the grandmother fading while we go at it raw
For clean incisions on polished clay—water spirit!
For the shapes of animals on our genitals
For the scab's child uncovering a mailbox rattlesnake
For the miracles tortillas wear on their faces
For the hole behind the net
    catching a cancerous neighbor's breath

For the murderer's first child, born retarded
For the little junkie-whore who does not repent
For the racehorse pumped full of painkillers
For the vasectomized man who raises as his own
    his wife's last child
For the man who keeps three wives and is faithful to them all
For the wife nearly ready to have children
For Japanese flags, blood on white tile, no children
For twin obese toddlers moaning for Twinkies
For two fingers sewn back to the drummer's hand
For the split decision of young girls bathing
For the stonewalled wife aiming into concrete
For carpets unvacuumed since he moved out
For the millionaire kneeling to edge his lawn
For the husband grateful beyond questions for his wife's return
For the horror of prayers, answered and answered
For the charango, the cuíca, the Día de los Muertos
For shards of flowerpots later mistaken
For the clear-headed moment lust recedes
For musky, bone-shattering novelty
For hundred-year-old letters uncommitted to the flames
For all the juices we can suck from one another
For the history of one hour's desire

HOW THEY ARE WITH EACH OTHER, THE WOMAN, THE MAN

They passed between them the huge
green coconut it took two hands to hold,
its skin smooth and cold against their palms.
They sipped up the milk, icy and blue,
through a pink straw, shaking out the last
drops on the sand so they could hurry
back to the man with the machete.

One whack and the cool world
opened like every sacred hollow
to offer more
of what they never knew
they wanted. The vendor splintered off
a thin curve of shell—rude spoon
to scoop out the creamy gel,
swirl it with salt, lemon,
chili, lift it to the tongue.

All morning their quarrels had circled—jagged
wings of frigate birds, prehistoric,
their great split tails
open Vs   no victory,
no peace. Spread legs. The impossibility
of blue. The woman.

The man. Each craving. They floated
in salt, ancient.
Not speaking. Pelicans rattled,
flung shattered water from their furry
heads. The woman, the man. Broken
waves, dream's hymen, bitter vow.

Green coconut, green
the punctured roundness
that slakes the body's
great thirst, green

the split husks
that invite us in,
the woman, the man
to the soul's
immense hunger

under
the sun's life-giving
cancerous grace.

WHAT TO COUNT ON

Not one star, not even the half moon
    on the night you were born
Not the flash of salmon
    nor ridges on blue snow
Not the flicker of raven's
    never-still eye
Not breath frozen in fine hairs
    beading the bull moose's nostril
Not one hand under flannel
    warming before reaching
Not burbot at home under Tanana ice
    not burbot pulled up into failing light
Not the knife blade honed, not the leather sheath
Not raw bawling in the dog yard
    when the musher barks *gee*
Not the gnawed ends of wrist-thick sticks
    mounded over beaver dens

Not solar flares scouring the earth over China
Not rime crystals bearding a sleek cheek of snow
Not six minutes more of darkness each day
Not air water food words touch

Not art
Not anything we expect
Not anything we expect to keep
Not anything we expect to keep us alive

Not the center of the sea
Not the birthplace of the waves
Not the compass too close to true north to guide us

Then with no warning
    flukes of three orcas
        rise, arc clear of sea water

HAUL ROAD

Twenty years ago,
primacord and front end loaders
uprooted this whole

watershed, loosened
dirt tied up
in root wads, blew

the ground's cover.
The dragline
scraped away

overburden
concealing coal
soon to be burnt

into electricity.
After trucking out
forty foot seams, twenty foot

seams, gleaned
skinny seams,
the miners

re-sculpted the hills,
broadcast
mixed seed from the air,

gave dust
dusty yellow
canola to hang onto until

willow and cranberry
reinvaded. Grown taller
than our pickup, good browse,

willow covers our tracks.
Hidden, your hard miner's palm
lifts from coal-colored lace

the sunwarmed hillside
of my breast, your mouth
seismic, turbulent

as we reclaim
one small patch,
August afternoon.

EACH RISE, EACH HOLLOW

You have taken me to a place
    where ripe papaya let go their stems
        and fell, heavy with juice, in our hands

You have taken me
    fifty feet under, swimming
        with eagle rays, while
            humpbacks above us
                sang their way south

You have shown me the ancient madrona
    healed over barbed wire
        nailed decades ago to red bark

You have held me shivering
    before a flaring
        crosshatch of split oak

In a small plane you have lifted me
    over the San Juans,
        all of us citizens of the clouds

You have taken me to a house
    with windows to the sky,
        walls open to night

You have made me your home

You have taken me to the place
    mist barely conceals the next island,
        where each rise, veiled, each hollow
            opens, sacred

WHAT WILL REMAIN

Lit from inside, birches
spark, flare,

blaze trails
for travelers

outstretched in air.
Tawny cranes

return to rest
where earth cradles water.

Cranes graze, pace, graze, then
flap scuttle jabber scold . . .

This harvest
flashes—wingspan of sand,

hillside of crook-necks
soon to move on.

What will remain
has always remained—

water seized
by ice-driven air,

faith through hard cold
that the languages

of marsh, sky,
sandhill crane

will keep on
with us or without.

YOUNG BOY DANCING AT PLAYA LOS MUERTOS

Had he been naked
as he skipped
shivering
out of the waves
we would not have known
he was so poor.

But he was not
naked. He wore
around his hips
an exhausted
pair of cast-off
underwear
gathered up at the hip,
secured
with the wire twist
from some tourist's
loaf of bread.

He shivered,
the edges of his lips
blue as the Virgin's veil.
Semana Santa, Holy Week, too early
really for perfect swimming.
Vendors hawked
Taxco silver, mangoes
on a stick, onyx seahorses
chiming, whole perch
skewered and seared.
His eyes swam after
the fish boy.

Timbales called out the guitarrón—
mariachis knocked Norteño beats
blanket to blanket up the beach.
The skinny one held on to his saggy
pants, elbowed close to sing along.
Someone else's fat papá lifted an eyebrow
in invitation, laughed, and together
man and boy danced a slick merengue,
flicked their hips ta-ta-ta,
swirled, one hand
suave against the belly,
the other a green rooster
kikiriki-ki
sunrise all day long!

The boy's whole body
told its truth—
he was not starving, no matter
what his ribs said. And his skin
could go ahead and offer the opinions
of its array of scars—no slash,
no welt, no still-healing burn
along his face, neck, shoulder
could talk louder
than the genius of his tiny
hips, those quick and playful
acts of God.

A CRACK IN THE BALANCED SHIP

Since you wish to be on the balanced ship,
I shall not push you off.
        —Telemachos

Bored with the perfect geometry of four legs,
four walls, all the right angles,
a young wife lives for the third part of the night
after stars balance heat and this raw-flesh age.

Thinking, she shakes the yoke:
marriage is salt, vital and basic;
mine, a salted mine
where promise catches light
but the miner comes home dirty.

Stroking the appalling softness below her belly
she splits into two sisters who can't stand to share
the same room. They agree to live on alternate days.

The river one, in love with casual water, sings,
What do you do with the other men
after you promise a husband?

The earth one, watching stars row past,
crafts a balanced ship
and does not give way.

CENSORED

Because we suspect
ourselves, knowing
what we're capable of, knowing

how thin the veneer,
wanting to control
what gets away from us

even now, with restraints
wrists, ankles,
our chastity belted down

so we can save ourselves
for and from. Because in our visions
our best moments

we all speak forbidden
languages. Because if anyone
knew us, really,

they could not
love us. This goes
for God, triple.

MAYBE

Maybe it's small, love—
ladybugs dotting driftwood at the tideline,
antique pelicans creaking over surf.

Maybe it's the unclipped
wings of wild plovers
stopping by the zoo's feeders

to stoke up
for the long flight north.
Maybe it's simple,

the elegant joining of your hip
gliding under my hand as we walk, listening
to our bodies, dream-charged drummers

sparking lightning in clear sky,
hearing the patter of glints
on seawater. Maybe love

lingers in marigolds luring the dead
back to reflect on the still pond, lingers
in heavy bread with a real crust to it.

SPAWN

Biting down, I take into myself
half-frozen herring eggs,
salty pops and crunches

tooth-strained off spruce boughs,
tar-tang of needles
sucked past the chill.

Inside me's their Inside Passage—
they hatch and school, return to spawn
in this milky way—vast briny tingle

of a lifetime's kisses—
all those refused
lingering on the tongue . . .

all those indulged, dissolved,
the sting on the skin, the spiny-edged
kelp-laden surf—

tiny explosions
of lives taken,
given, on the incoming tide.

CHENA NIGHT

The cow moose with twin calves
swims our river, rises dripping
in the scant dark of August.

They crop broccoli
ground level, take one bite
of each cabbage.

Rhubarb they leave,
and zucchini. Nightshade
leaves survive.

Before dawn, the river
covers their tracks.

Wherever they brush the trees,
leaves turn gold.

ANNIVERSARY

What being nests
        in our hollows?

What being nests
        in our broken places?

Bound, one self
        rising into two

who year after year
        stick around, stay

Testament, new
        each morning, each day

What whorl
        borne of both of us

peels loose?
        What world

borne of both of us
        lifts away?

THE RUN OF SILVERS

If, inside me,
his one cell swam among millions
as if it knew the way,
met the ripe star falling
through my thick clouded sky

then plunged in headlong
renouncing even the tail that allowed it
to make the swim,

then I will tell our new
daughter or son, the one
taking shape, taking over
inside and out
that one afternoon

a run of silvers surged
through Resurrection Bay,
such hurry toward death!
Their potent ballet—muscular
dazzling leaps into the blinding
sparkle of an air they can't breathe—

how they hovered
in blue air—angels, perhaps,
messengers surely

sent to nourish and teach
those of us who might listen . . .

They did not know where
they were going,
they simply found their way.

We did not catch our supper that day.
Glacial spray from the crashing falls
chilled our faces, cleared our eyes.

In never-ending daylight
sea otters rocked
belly up on the incoming
tide, swallowing whole
blue mussels
stone pounded
against their chests.

We never had touched each other
in quite such tender danger.

AGAIN, AGAIN

As I'm waking you drift

your stiffening cock

up the back of my knee.

Just born as we touch

our new bodies can't wait to laugh.

Only for a few reasons,

all holy,

do people kneel.

Against my cheek your thighs open

open, wings moist

from the other world

Both my hands, very wet, stroke . . .

Let the mouths be jealous

a little while

You behind me

blind rhino

crashing through brush

I bounce out overripe red flame

grapes for the jays

then wait naked among them

The elegant herons

our long kisses

My nipples between

your teeth—

when the pain turns

exquisite, I fill

your hand

with spring water.

                                        Watching me touch

                                        myself you

                                        become a woman

Brace yourself! Bright open lips

swoop down on your kiss

What fine tuning you do, twisting

my nipples, you about ready

in my mouth

After months holding back, you bend

my head forward and nip

the nape of my neck

What deaths do we face

when we refuse

SPRING

Botticelli never pictured
breakup boots, black ice,
red pickup

hauled back up
the bank after falling through.
A few days' sun.

All on one
day, the leaves. Open,
open and open.

Marbled gold
pollen floats.
Every year

since it was a river, this.
Upstream an ice dam
groans, screams,

scrapes. Gives.
Whole new breakup—
huge floes blunder

downriver, gouge up
whole trees. Gossamer
river—crushed ice

shushes, slushes,
three days
floating by.

SUMMER

No need to leave the light on,
just open one eye
and the world enters
you, sprawled atop
clean sheets, your torso
shadowed
by mine.

Sunlight all day, all night,
so when we wake,
no way to tell
whether anyone else
exists or whether this
new day, if it is day,
means for us to rise.

Touched, our bodies
blaze awake, dawn
on us, shine.
Tongues trace
rivers of light
surging inside
us, outside of time.

AUTUMN

Higher than sandhill cranes
turned south, we fly
one last time this season

north. Wayward breezes
lift us. Outlined yellow
each creek, each draw.

Dryer hillsides
brush ruddy tundra.
Beyond the Yukon,

past the tors
no storm has scoured away,
the sky turns

gray angora.
We bank and soar
back toward home

skim down on the float pond
filled with marvels we've been given
to see, suffused with grace.

Hard frost tonight—
the world
changes its mind.

WINTER

Hip deep in heaped snow
birches sway.

By their example, we know
the alpenglow will one day rise,

the sun limping now
will lift itself higher

and stay a little longer.
Sun on the birches'

broken places, sun
on wounds, on scars . . .

Winter sun showing us
our shadows

contain colors
we barely dream of . . .

WIDE ICY RIVER

How, driving in whiteout
        above tree line, the summit
                road washed white, blue white
                      gone to swirling powder, we gasp
                            whirling inside the frosted sigh

of the earth.
        Straining in whiteout
                our eyes the eyes of creatures
                      unsuited to this element
                            vestigial, liquid ornaments

splashing for flashes of orange.
        Each marker hovers,
                flicks past too
                      fast, we can't let it go, we can't
                            see it or the next—

beyond our tiny sphere, the expanse—
    white on white, the endless
        domes of our unknowing.
            Our knowing
                what we cannot see

could very well whisk away
    our visible breath.

How the ones we loved
        well enough
                or not
                        would miss us with a white-hot
                                burning for as long as they

held on. And those who
        held old photographs
                would conjure our voices
                        above tree line, in whiteout,
                              the road drifted over.

Long after the photos
        have fallen, white
                flakes of ash
                        in a stranger's grate,
                              our distant, white-boned

daughter will warm her cold
        ear along the thigh of her lover.
                Her breath on his skin
                        white language
                              he can lose himself in

that white
        on white
                remake us
                        windswept blue
                              in its own image.

BLAZE

Last season's snow's slipped
back into sky. Red willow
branches broken by

browsing moose calves'
golden blond gambol
splay, unravel.

Frayed filaments
nipped then swallowed
travel now, transformed,

gangly moose muscle.
Bog weeds soon to be
fast under ice

ripple, sway.
Our flesh past its prime,
unsteady, quickens.

Blue blaze—
beyond any map.
More than one life-

time's gash, white bark
barked, love's deep
continent not yet

surveyed. One breath,
two. Fresh snow in the air,
not fallen.

THE LONGEST NIGHT OF THE YEAR

Before contact, dancers around here
wore masks, carved parts of trees
into faces that revealed
what their own
covered up.

After days, after
long nights drumming,
chanting, raising hands, raising
voices to the sky,
dancers turned
their second faces
back to the earth,
left them to weather.
That whole day lit
only by gauzy green
aurora, the boreal
forest holding
still under snow.
Unmarked, the path
of the sun
among stars.

A century later, birch trees
mark a turning point—
more light every day
after this day.
A century later, birch trees
carve solstice riddles.

What face should we put on
for ceremonies? What face
should we wear every day?

With the sun so far away
how do we know
where to turn?

With our roots well covered,
our branches bare,
what are we?

Every night a face returns
to earth. Every morning
a new face is born.
What are we?

The answers
paper birch bark
whispers.

In stillness
paper birch bark peels.

Blaze Art by Kesler Woodward

Graces, page 12
Oil on canvas
48" x 90"
Private collection, Fairbanks, Alaska

A Sapling for Heather, page 14
Acrylic on board
7" x 5"
Private collection, Anchorage, Alaska

Couple, page 16
Oil on canvas
60" x 24"
Private collection, Fairbanks, Alaska

Untitled #6, page 18
Oil on canvas
60" x 84"

Bright Birches in Winter, page 20
Oil on canvas
60" x 84"
Collection of the artist

Melt, page 22
Oil on canvas
60" x 24"
Private collection, Denver, Colorado

Birch Portrait #19, page 24
Oil on canvas
48" x 60"
Charlotte Athletic Club, Charlotte, North Carolina

Birch Bark, St. Matthew, page 26
Oil pastel on paper
28" x 40"
C. B. Bettisworth Architects, Fairbanks, Alaska

Birch Portrait #30, page 28
Oil on canvas
48" x 60"
Private collection, Fairbanks, Alaska

Birch Portrait, Homer, page 30
Oil pastel on paper
40" x 28"

Birch Portrait #33, page 32
Oil on canvas
48" x 60"
Private collection, Homer, Alaska

Bright Birch, Deep Winter, page 34
Oil on canvas
60" x 84"
Private collection, Augusta, Georgia

Untitled #4, page 36
Oil on paper
22" x 30"
Private collection, Anchorage, Alaska

Bright Birch, page 38
Oil on canvas
72" x 18"
Private collection, Fairbanks, Alaska

Little Gidding, page 40
Acrylic on canvas
48" x 60"
British Petroleum, Anchorage, Alaska

Spring Green, page 42
Acrylic on canvas
72" x 60"
University of Alaska Museum

Birch Portrait #29, page 44
Oil on paper
30" x 22"
Private collection, Anchorage, Alaska

Birch Portrait #35, page 46
Oil on canvas
84" x 60"

Summer Birch, page 48
Oil on board
12" x 9"
Private collection, Fairbanks, Alaska

Birch Portrait #32, page 50
Oil on canvas
60" x 48"

Chena Birch, page 52
Oil on board
12" x 9"
Private collection, Fairbanks, Alaska

Bright Birch #2, page 54
Oil pastel on paper
40" x 32"

Birch Portrait #31, page 56
Oil on canvas
60" x 48"

First Snow, September, page 58
Oil on canvas
49" x 51"
Private collection, Fairbanks, Alaska

Northern September, page 60
Acrylic on canvas
49" x 36"
Private collection, Fairbanks, Alaska

September Light, page 62
Oil on canvas
48" x 36"
Private collection, Charlotte, North Carolina

Birch Portrait #64, page 64
Oil on canvas
48" x 36"
Private collection, Anchorage, Alaska

Triple Birch Portrait, page 66
Oil on canvas
48" x 60"
Private collection, Hilton Head, South Carolina

Burnt Norton, page 68
Acrylic on canvas
48" x 60"
C.B. Bettisworth Architects, Fairbanks, Alaska

Birch Portrait #22, page 70
Oil on canvas
60" x 84"
Private collection, Fairbanks, Alaska

Birch Portrait #62, page 72
Oil on canvas
36" x 24"
Morris Communications Company, Augusta, Georgia

Birch Portrait #20, page 74
Oil on canvas
48" x 60"

Birch Portrait #61, page 76
Acrylic on board
24" x 36"
Private collection, Fairbanks, Alaska

Seasons of Praise: Spring, page 78, 134
Oil on canvas
87" x 36"
Holy Family Chapel, Fairbanks, Alaska

Seasons of Praise: Summer, page 78, 136
Oil on canvas
87" x 36"
Holy Family Chapel, Fairbanks, Alaska

Seasons of Praise: Autumn, page 79, 138
Oil on canvas
87" x 36"
Holy Family Chapel, Fairbanks, Alaska

Seasons of Praise: Winter, page 79, 140
Oil on canvas
87" x 36"
Holy Family Chapel, Fairbanks, Alaska

Bright Birch #3, page 80
Oil pastel on paper
40" x 28"

Bold Birch, page 82
3-color original lithograph
31" x 24"
Edition of 15

Chimera, page 84
Acrylic on canvas
40" x 60"
Private collection, Fairbanks, Alaska

Little Birch Portrait, page 86
Oil on board
12" x 9"
Private collection, Fairbanks, Alaska

Birch Portrait #18, page 88
Oil on canvas
48" x 60"
Xerox Corporation, Anchorage, Alaska

Snow Up On Birches, page 90
Acrylic on canvas
24" x 20"
Morris Communications Company, Augusta, Georgia

Harriman Birches, page 92
Oil on canvas
30" x 84"
Collection of the artist

Bright Birch #1, page 94
Oil pastel on paper
40" x 82"
Private collection, Charlotte, North Carolina

Woods at Creamer's, page 96
Acrylic on canvas
48" x 60"
University of Alaska Museum

Birch Portrait #50, page 98
Oil on canvas
48" x 54"

Birch Portrait #15, page 100
Oil on canvas
60" x 84"
Private collection, Salem, Oregon

Fall Fever, page 102
Acrylic on canvas
48" x 48"
Private collection, Anchorage, Alaska

Bright Birch #4, page 104
Oil pastel on paper
40" x 28"

Birch Portrait #41, page 106
Oil on paper
22" x 30"

Birch Portrait #10, page 108
Oil on paper
22" x 30"

Birch Portrait #25, page 110
Oil on paper
22" x 30"
Private collection, Anchorage, Alaska

Birch Portrait #45, page 112
Oil on paper
22" x 30"
Private collection, Anchorage, Alaska

Chase's Woods, page 114
Oil on board
18" x 24"
Private collection, Fairbanks, Alaska

Anniversary, page 116
Oil on canvas
60" x 84"
Private collection, Pensacola, Florida

Birch Portrait #14, page 118
Oil on canvas
60" x 84"
Private collection, Anchorage, Alaska

New Fires, page 120
Oil on canvas
60" x 84"
Private collection, Anchorage, Alaska

Birch Portrait #17, page 122
Oil on canvas
48" x 60"
Private collection, Anchorage, Alaska

Birch Portrait #21, page 124
Oil on canvas
60" x 84"
Private collection, Anchorage, Alaska

Birch Portrait #28, page 126
Oil on paper
30" x 22"
Private collection, Anchorage, Alaska

Birch Portrait #47, page 128
Oil on paper
22" x 30"
Guest Quarters Hotel, Bethesda, Maryland

Tanana Birch Portrait, page 130
Oil on canvas
48" x 60"
Private collection, Charlotte, North Carolina

Blue Bark Peels, page 132
Oil on canvas
48" x 60"
Private collection, Eugene, Oregon

Close Set Birches, page 142
Oil on canvas
60" x 84"
Federal Reserve Bank, Richmond, Virginia

Birch Portrait #34, page 144
Oil on canvas
60" x 84"
Private collection, Fairbanks, Alaska

East Coker, page 146
Acrylic on canvas
48" x 36"
Private collection, Reno, Nevada

Birch Portrait #1, page 148
Acrylic on canvas
60" x 44"
Anchorage Museum of History and Art

Acknowledgments, Art

I extend my grateful thanks to the many individuals and institutions who have supported me by acquiring the paintings reproduced in this volume. I have respected the privacy of the individuals and have noted only the institutions in the list of works depicted.

Thank you to Wanda Chin, who helped us begin to envision a form for this collaboration.

Thank you to Mark Cull and Kate Gale of Red Hen Press.

Thank you so much to Peggy Shumaker and Joe Usibelli.

And thanks above all to my wife Missy and our son Eli, for your love and support.

Acknowledgments, poetry

Grateful thanks to the editors of the publications where these poems first appeared, sometimes in earlier versions:

Alaska Quarterly Review, The American Poetry Review, Ascent, Bellingham Review, Blackbird, Caprice, Crab Orchard Review, Flyway, Hayden's Ferry Review, In The Eye of the Beholder, The James River Review, Looking North, New Virginia Review, Nimrod, The Northern Review, Permafrost, Ploughshares, Poetry Kantu (Japan), Prairie Schooner, Puerto del Sol, Third Coast, Weber Studies

Some of these poems were selected from earlier collections:

Esperanza's Hair (Alabama)
The Circle of Totems (Pitt)
Wings Moist from the Other World (Pitt)
Underground Rivers (Red Hen)

Thank you to Wanda Chin, who helped us see what this book could be.
Thanks to Kes, Missy, and Eli Woodward.
Many thanks to Kate Gale and Mark Cull.

Thanks beyond measure to Joe Usibelli.

Biographical note ~ Peggy Shumaker

Peggy Shumaker was born in La Mesa, California, and grew up in Tucson, Arizona. She earned her BA and MFA in Creative Writing from the University of Arizona. For many years she was writer in residence for the Arizona Commission on the Arts, working with school children, prison inmates, honors students, deaf adults, teen parents, gang members, library patrons, and the elderly.

Peggy Shumaker's books of poems include *Underground Rivers* (Red Hen Press), *Wings Moist from the Other World*, *The Circle of Totems*, *Braided River*, and *Esperanza's Hair*. Her nonfiction has appeared in *Short Takes: Brief Encounters with Contemporary Nonfiction* (Norton), *A Road of Her Own* (Fulcrum), *Under Northern Lights* (U. WA Press), *A Year in Place* (U. UT Press), *Prairie Schooner* and *Ascent*.

Shumaker has won a poetry fellowship from the National Endowment for the Arts, and several awards for teaching. She served as poet in residence at the Stadler Center for Poetry at Bucknell and as President of the Board of Directors of the Associated Writing Programs. Professor emerita from University of Alaska Fairbanks, Shumaker was Chair of the English Department and Director of the MFA program in Creative Writing. She currently teaches in the low-residency Rainier Writing Workshop. Peggy Shumaker and her husband Joe Usibelli live in Fairbanks, Alaska, and travel widely.

Biographical note ~ Kesler Woodward

Kesler Woodward was born in Aiken, South Carolina in 1951. He and his wife Missy live in LaConner, Washington, where they are partners in Braarud/Woodward Fine Art. They were Alaska residents from 1977 through 2004.

Woodward served as Curator of Visual Arts at the Alaska State Museum and as Artistic Director of the Visual Arts Center of Alaska before moving to Fairbanks in 1981. He is currently Professor of Art, Emeritus at the University of Alaska Fairbanks, where he taught for two decades, serving as Chair of the Art Department and as Chair of the Division of Arts and Communications. He currently serves on the board of the Alaska Arts and Culture Foundation and on the board of trustees of the Western States Arts Federation.

Woodward's paintings are included in all major public art collections in Alaska, and in museum, corporate and private collections on both coasts of the United States. Solo exhibits to his credit include the Morris Museum of Art, University of Alaska Museum, Alaska State Museum, Anchorage Museum of History and Art, and public and commercial galleries throughout the U.S. Juried and invitational exhibitions including his work have ranged from Alaska to Brazil and Russia.

Also an art historian and curator, Woodward since 1990 has published six books on Alaskan art, including the first comprehensive survey of the fine arts in Alaska, *Painting in the North*, published by the Anchorage Museum and University of Washington Press in 1993. His latest volume, *A Northern Adventure: The Art of Fred Machetanz*, was published in May, 2004. He has lectured on art of the circumpolar north from Alaska to Georgia, New England, and the British Museum in London.

In October, 2004, Kesler Woodward received the Alaska Governor's Art Award for Lifetime Achievement.